THERAPIST
COLORING BOOK

THIS BOOK BELONGS TO:

____

____

I Workout
Other
PEOPLE'S
Problems

I Used to have a
LIFE
but i decided to be a
THERAPIST

I'm a
Therapist
what's your
SUPER
POWER?

KEEP
TALKING
I'M
DIAGNOSING
YOU!

DON'T
MAKE ME
USE MY
THERAPIST
VOICE!

I'm not in
The Mood
for
TALKING
I'm here to
LISTEN

I'm a Therapist!
Nothing
SCARES
ME!

YODA BEST
THERAPIST!

YES, I M A
THERAPIST
BUT
I CAN NOT
FIX STUPID

I Can Talk
You Into
ANYTHING

49% Therapist
51% Badass

Being a
THERAPIST
Is Easy
IT'S LIKE RIDING A BIKE
EXCEPT THE BIKE
Is On Fire
YOU'RE ON FIRE
EVERYTHING IS ON FIRE!

I'm Silently Analyzing your Gait

LOOK AT YOU
BECOMING
A THERAPIST
AND
Shit!

WORLD'S
Okayest
THERAPIST!

Changing
Lives
One Session
at a Time

Therapist
I'll Be There
For You!

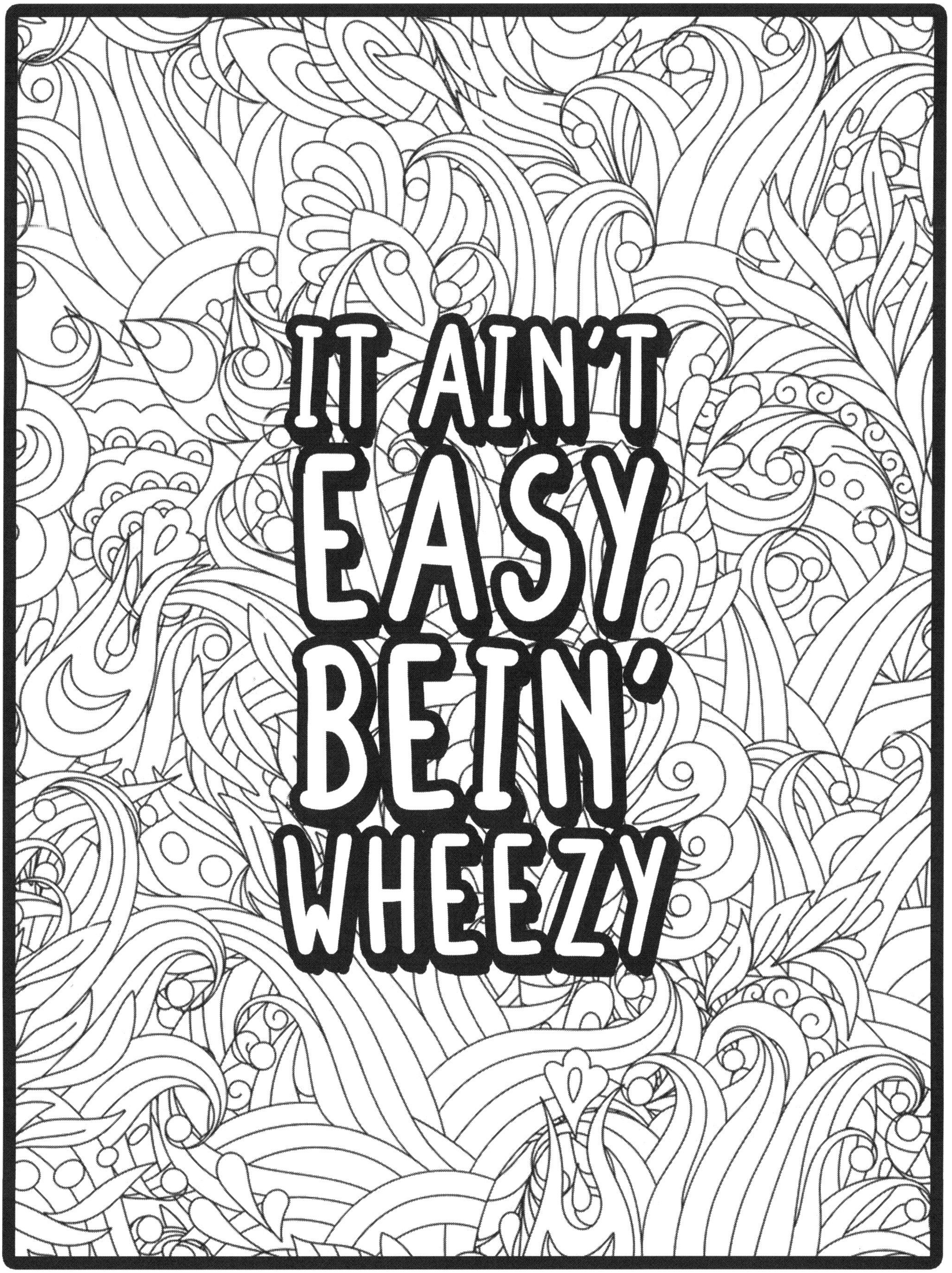
IT AIN'T
EASY
BEIN'
WHEEZY

LIFE IS
Better
WITH
MASSAGE!

THIS IS WHAT
AN AWESOME
THERAPIST
LOOKS LIKE

Manufactured by Amazon.ca
Bolton, ON

21726238R00024